T0024614

Kids Who Are Changing the World

by Sheila Sweeny Higginson

illustrated by Alyssa Petersen

Ready-to-Read

Simon Spotlight
New York London Toronto Sydney New Delhi

SIMON SPOTLIGHT

An imprint of Simon & Schuster Children's Publishing Division
1230 Avenue of the Americas, New York, New York 10020
This Simon Spotlight edition March 2019
Text copyright © 2019 by Simon & Schuster, Inc.
Illustrations copyright © 2019 by Alyssa Petersen
All rights reserved, including the right of reproduction in whole or in part in any form.
SIMON SPOTLIGHT, READY-TO-READ, and colophon are registered trademarks of Simon & Schuster, Inc.
For information about special discounts for bulk purchases, please contact Simon & Schuster
Special Sales at 1-866-506-1949 or business@simonandschuster.com.
Manufactured in the United States of America 0521 LAK
6 8 10 9 7
Library of Congress Cataloging-in-Publication Data
Names: Higginson, Sheila Sweeny, 1966- author. | Petersen, Alyssa, illustrator.
Title: Kids who are changing the world! / by Sheila Sweeny Higginson ; illustrated by Alyssa Petersen.
Description: First edition. | New York : Simon Spotlight, 2018. | Series: You should meet | Audience: Age 6–8.
Identifiers: LCCN 2018031340 (print) | LCCN 2018046030 (eBook) |
ISBN 9781534432161 (eBook) | ISBN 9781534432147 (pbk) | ISBN 9781534432154 (hc)
Subjects: LCSH: Child volunteers—Juvenile literature. | Children as inventors—Juvenile literature. | Children
and the environment—Juvenile literature.
Classification: LCC HQ784.V64 (eBook) | LCC HQ784.V64 H54 2018 (print) | DDC 333.7083—dc23
LC record available at https://lccn.loc.gov/2018031340

CONTENTS

Introduction

The world is a big place, and it is filled with amazing people and places. It also has many problems. Some of those problems are challenging. Even grown-ups have a hard time figuring out how to solve them. So how can one kid do it? Is it really possible for a kid like you to change the world?

An African proverb says, "If you think you're too small to make a difference, you haven't spent the night with a mosquito." The kids in this book know that you're never too small to start changing the world!

Chapter 1
Meet Jahkil Naeem Jackson

Jahkil Naeem Jackson was only five years old when he learned about a problem in his community. Jahkil's aunt took him to help hand out soup and chili to people in Chicago who were homeless. He said that he saw how they lived with rats and sleeping bags on the concrete and wanted to help in some way ever since.

Jahkil wished he could buy or build a home for every person who needed one. That would be a lot of homes—too many for one boy to build. One recent study showed that in Chicago, thousands of people live without a home. And more than half a million (500,000) people in the United States are homeless on a typical night.

The problem of homelessness is huge and complicated. Jahkil didn't let that stop him from finding a way to help. He knew he couldn't build houses yet, but he could fill bags.

When Jahkil was eight, he started making **blessing bags** for homeless people. "The stuff that's in the blessing bags are tissues, soap, water, deodorant," Jahkil explained. "Usually stuff that can help them in their everyday activities."

At first, Jahkil made a few hundred bags. He filled up the bags with the help of his friends, his family, and his classmates at Ray Elementary School. Then they put the bags into his godfather's truck and headed off to hand them out.

Those first trips only made Jahkil want to do even more. With the help of his family, Jahkil started a foundation called **Project I Am**. Now he works with other groups in the community so he can get blessing bags into even more hands.

In 2017, when Jahkil was ten, he decided he wanted to give out five thousand blessing bags. He reached his goal and more! Some of Jahkil's blessing bags went far beyond Chicago to hurricane survivors in Florida, Texas, and Puerto Rico, and to orphans in Swaziland, Africa.

Former president Barack Obama heard about Jahkil's work and wrote about him on social media. "All across America, people chose to get involved, get engaged, and stand up. Each of us can make a difference, and all of us ought to try," he wrote after telling people about Jahkil's blessing bags.

For his work, Jahkil received an award that is given to twenty-five young people a year who are making a positive difference in the world. He was honored with the 2017 Gloria Barron Prize for Young Heroes, along with five thousand dollars that he put into Project I Am. Jahkil was beyond excited to receive such an honor.

"I went screaming all the way from my room and back to the living room," he told his hometown newspaper, the *Chicago Tribune*.

"I want to make sure people in need aren't just unknown," he added. "I think homeless people—most people don't recognize them and walk past them and drive past them. I want to let people know that homeless people are people too."

Jahkil hasn't given up on his dream of building houses for the homeless either. He learned about a program in Detroit that builds tiny homes for the homeless. He wants to help get a movement like that started in Chicago.

"I want to build one with my bare hands," Jahkil told a reporter. "I want to see how that feels."

He also wants to get more kids in more cities to make their own blessing bags. Jahkil and his parents created starter kits that they send to schools and groups through the Project I Am website. The site says it costs about nine dollars to make each blessing bag. Jahkil wants every kid to understand what he's learned. You don't have to wait until you're an adult to be great—you can be great now!

Do you want to help with the problem of homelessness, like Jahkil does? You can join his blessing bag mission. You can do other things too. Here are a few ideas:

• With the help of a parent or caregiver, donate clothes you don't need to a local shelter. (They should be clean and in good condition.)

• Ask your friends to bring various food items (or supplies for blessing bags) to your birthday party instead of presents. Then donate them to a local homeless shelter.

• Start a food drive in your class or school and send the food to a local food kitchen.

Chapter 2
Meet Natalie Hampton

The problem of bullying is personal to Natalie Hampton, because she was a victim of it. The bullying that Natalie went through started with five simple words: "You can't sit with us."

When Natalie started a new school in seventh grade, she thought it would be easy to make new friends. She soon found out she was wrong. She didn't fit in. Her classmates were not just unfriendly—they were mean. "You'll never have any friends," kids told her.

Natalie isn't alone. Research shows that about one in three US students in grades six through twelve have experienced  bullying. Being a victim of bullying can make you sad, nervous, and anxious.

Natalie began to have stomachaches and nightmares. She started to lose hope that life would ever get better.

Finally, after two very tough years, Natalie transferred to a new school. There, as she tells it, one student made all the difference.

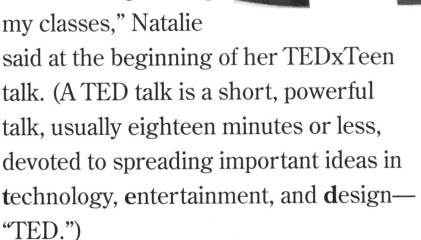

"A boy stopped me in my school hallway to ask me if I needed help finding my classes," Natalie said at the beginning of her TEDxTeen talk. (A TED talk is a short, powerful talk, usually eighteen minutes or less, devoted to spreading important ideas in technology, entertainment, and design—"TED.")

When that boy offered to help Natalie, that's when she learned that a simple act of kindness can make a difference in someone's life. It only took that one student to change hers.

Natalie could have just moved on in her new school with her new friends. But she knew the problem was bigger than just her experience. She wanted to help solve it.

Natalie believed that eating lunch alone was a symbol of how isolating bullying can be. At her new school, she invited other students who were sitting alone to her table.

"Even though I was easily able to help the kids within my own school community," Natalie said, "I wanted to do something more."

She started to think of ideas to help with the problem. She didn't really know how to code, but she decided that creating an app would be the best way to get the message to a large number of kids. Natalie started drawing ideas in a notebook. Then she worked with a professional coder to create the app. After months of testing, Natalie's app, called **Sit With Us**, was ready to meet the digital world.

SIT WITH US

Sit With Us is a free mobile app that helps kids find other kids to sit with at lunch. Students download it onto their phones. Some can become ambassadors. They are the ones who invite anyone who doesn't have a place to sit to join them. Through the app, students look for ambassadors so they don't have to sit alone at lunch.

Because it's private and all done through the phone, none of the other students know who is asking, and the students looking for a place to sit know that they won't be rejected.

Natalie's idea—
and her app—spread
like wildfire. More
than a hundred
thousand people
are using Sit
With Us in at least
eight countries around
the world.

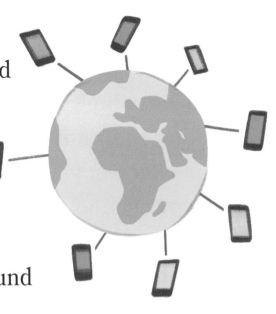

Natalie was named one of the most
influential teen social entrepreneurs who
have found a solution
or idea to address a
basic human need.
She won an award
from the United
Nations Youth
Assembly, and
got to deliver a
speech in the
UN's General
Assembly Hall.

At the end of her TEDxTeen talk, Natalie said, "All it takes is one person to change the world, and that person—starting right now—is you."

So what can you do to make the world, and your school, a kinder place?

You can start by taking Natalie's lead at lunchtime. If you see a kid sitting alone, ask him or her to join you.

It's important to treat everyone with kindness and respect. Here's how:

• Think about what you say. If you know it would hurt someone's feelings, even if they're not a friend, or not in the room, don't say it.
• Remember that everyone is different. That doesn't mean they're better, or worse, just different. Respect that.
• If you see someone being bullied, you don't have to confront the bully. Just interrupt. Talk to the victim, even if he or she isn't a friend, and help them get out of the situation by inviting them to join you.

Chapter 3
Meet Gitanjali Rao

What problem do you think America's top scientists could solve? Gitanjali Rao isn't a professional scientist—yet. She's still a kid! But when Gitanjali learned about the water crisis in Flint, Michigan, she saw a problem that she believed she could help solve.

The situation with Flint's water supply started with a money problem. While officials were working on a solution, the city started getting water from the Flint River. Soon, people in the town began to notice the funny smell, look, and taste of the water.

The water was tested by a government agency, and dangerous levels of lead were found. When people, especially kids, take in lead through drinking water, there can be serious health effects.

Gitanjali doesn't live in Flint. She doesn't even live in the state of Michigan. Still, she followed the story closely. People were using test strips to check their drinking water for lead. A test strip has different colors on it. Each color represents a certain mineral. When it is dipped in water, if the lead content is too high, the color will change on the strip. When she saw her parents using test strips to check their own water for lead, she got an idea. Test strips can give quick results, but they aren't always the best results. More accurate testing can cost up to a hundred dollars, and it has to be sent to a lab. Gitanjali knew that the high price of testing could stop many people from learning the truth about their drinking water.

"I love to innovate and invent new technology," Gitanjali said. "I like finding solutions to real problems." That's just what she did. Gitanjali started with carbon nanotube sensors. They're made out of a tube-shaped material that is about ten thousand times thinner than a human hair. Gitanjali used them to build a device that can detect lead in water more quickly and more accurately than other methods. Gitanjali's device works with a smartphone app, so people can see the results right away.

Gitanjali called her device "Tethys." She named it after the Greek goddess of fresh water. It makes water testing cheaper, easier, and more accurate, so that more people can take action if there is a problem with their water supply.

Most scientists work for many years to get to the top of their field. Gitanjali was named America's Top Young Scientist when she was only eleven years old! She received a twenty-five-thousand-dollar prize that can help her develop her work.

"Just have fun with science and keep digging deep for solutions," she advises kids who are interested in changing the world through science. "If you do not succeed the first time, that's okay! There is never a limit to the number of tries it takes to accomplish a goal."

Water isn't just a problem in Flint, Michigan. More than two billion people around the world lack access to clean drinking water at home. It's a big problem, but you already know that you're big enough to make a difference, right?

What can you do?

• First, like Gitanjali, learn about the water crisis in your area or around the world. The more you know, the better you'll be at helping.

• Next, understand that even if it's easy for you to get water, it's a limited resource. Think about your water footprint. That's the amount of fresh water you use. There are simple ways you can reduce it, like turning off the faucet while you brush your teeth, or taking shorter showers.

• Remind your friends to be more careful and not waste water.

Chapter 4
Meet Joris Hutchison

It's not surprising that the problem Joris Hutchison decided to help with involves cheetahs. They've been his favorite animals since he was six years old.

"When I was six, I was reading a book that said that cheetahs might become extinct in my lifetime," Joris said. "I didn't know what that meant."

Joris's mom explained what the word "extinct" meant. (**Extinction** of a particular animal happens when there are no more individuals of that species alive anywhere in the world.) Joris became really sad when he realized that cheetahs might soon die out and the species could disappear completely from the planet.

"I asked my mom what I could do to help," Joris said. "And that's when I got involved in cheetah conservation."

Wildlife conservation is the work that people do to protect plant and animal species in their natural habitats. Joris isn't the only person who believes the fastest land mammals on earth are worth saving. In African countries like Namibia, organizations have been working to keep cheetahs from becoming extinct.

Joris started at home. He sold lemonade, flowers, and T-shirts, and organized skating parties and a garage sale. He raised more than fourteen thousand dollars! Then he used that 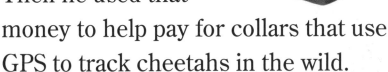 money to help pay for collars that use GPS to track cheetahs in the wild.

Joris donates his money, and his time, to N/a'an ku sê (NON-koo-say). It's one of the wildlife conservation organizations in Namibia.

LEMONADE $1

In the summer, Joris travels to Namibia with his mom to volunteer at N/a'an ku sê's sanctuary. He helps get the cheetah's food ready and clean out the area where they live.

At N/a'an ku sê, they also work to teach farmers about the importance of cheetahs. They convince them to help put collars on the cheetahs instead of killing them. The collars can show the farmers that the cheetahs aren't actually hurting their farm animals. Because of this work, farmers have created safe zones for cheetahs.

Like Jahkil, Joris was honored with the 2017 Gloria Barron Prize for Young Heroes. Can you guess what he did with the five-thousand-dollar prize? He donated it to N/a'an ku sê, of course!

Joris wants to be a wildlife biologist when he grows up, and to work at N/a'an ku sê.

"I've learned that everyone can make a difference, even if you're just a kid," Joris said. "You just have to start somewhere!"

You can make a difference for endangered animals around the world too. Here are some ideas:

• Find a local conservation society or organization. Learn about a local problem that you can do something about.

• Speak out about topics that protect wildlife, such as ivory bans. Even small voices can be loud when they join together.

• Reduce the amount of plastic you use. Recycle and reuse it too! Plastic takes hundreds of years to break down. The less we can use, the better.

BUT WAIT. . .

THERE'S MORE!

In this book, you've met some incredible kids who are changing the world. Read on to learn about more amazing kids, the science behind kindness, and about the different types of conservation!

Young Inventors in History

Louis Braille was only three years old when he was blinded by an accident. In the 1800s blind children learned to read by tracing raised-print letters with their fingers. While in school, Louis met Charles Barbier, who had developed a code with raised dots so that French soldiers could read messages at night with their fingers, without having to turn on a light. Louis spent three years—from age twelve to fifteen—further improving and developing Barbier's system, until he finally created the Braille code. Now, thousands of blind people use Braille to read.

In the 1800s many children worked in factories to help their parents make an income. **Margaret Knight** was one of them. At only twelve years old, she had to leave school to work in a cotton mill. There, she witnessed a young worker get injured by one of the machines. To improve safety, Margaret invented a device that would prevent these kinds of injuries from happening in the future. Her inventing did not stop there—Margaret created toys for her brothers and sisters, a clasp for robes, a dress and a lining to protect a skirt from wrinkles, and the folded paper bag we use in grocery stores today! She is now known as "Lady Edison" for her great inventions and contributions.

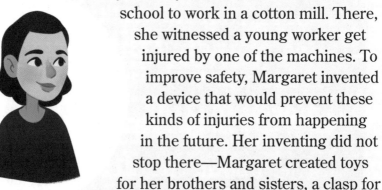

The Science of Kindness

Did you know being kind isn't just good for others? It's also good for you!

• When you're kind—whether it's inviting someone to eat lunch with you or simply holding the door open for someone—your brain releases a chemical called **serotonin**. Serotonin is a feel-good chemical in your brain that makes you happy!

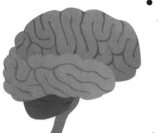

• Being kind is also contagious. When you witness someone else performing an act of kindness, another chemical in your brain is released. This is called **oxytocin**, which helps improve your overall heart health!

• If you're feeling tired, try being kind! According to some studies, people feel stronger and more energetic after helping others!

• Parents always tell their kids that eating well and exercising make us live longer. But did you know that you can also increase your life span by giving to others? Studies show that volunteering and giving to others improve overall health—meaning you could live longer!

• When you're feeling stressed, your brain releases a hormone called **cortisol**. But as you help others, this hormone is reduced in your body, meaning you feel less stressed! Participating in or witnessing acts of kindness also produces **endorphins** (the brain's painkiller), which reduce anxiety and sadness.

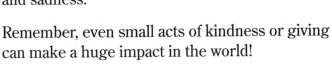

Remember, even small acts of kindness or giving can make a huge impact in the world!

Tips on Being Kind

• Don't be kind just to get something out of it. Kindness is all about caring genuinely for those around you and wanting the best for them. The greatest acts of kindness come from those who expect nothing in return.

• Be kind to yourself. We are often too involved in helping others to take the time to be kind to ourselves. Ask yourself what you can do to feel better, and practice! When you have a negative thought, replace it with a positive one. You can also practice saying nice things you like about yourself in the mirror!

• Be kind to everyone, not just those in need. It's great to help those less fortunate than ourselves, but it's also important to help those who aren't in obvious need. You never know what someone is going through at home or at school, so be kind to everyone around you.

Conservation

Conservation means the "careful preservation and protection of something." Like the kids you met in this book, there are several ways you can help protect and conserve things you care about. The most common types of conservation are:

Water conservation is the practice of using water efficiently to reduce unnecessary water usage and save water. Did you know that less than 1 percent of the earth's water supply is fresh, drinkable water? The rest of the water is salt water found in the ocean, or frozen water we can't drink. This means the seven and a half billion people on earth are sharing a very small amount of water! Therefore, it is important to use water wisely. Here are some ways you can reduce your water usage:

• Turn off the tap! Don't leave the water running when doing common things like brushing your teeth, washing your hands, or scrubbing the dishes. Even turning it off for a few minutes per day will save hundreds of gallons of water every year!

• Take shorter showers. We all love the warmth of a shower, but staying in there while the water is running is wasting several gallons of water. Try timing yourself next time you're in the shower—can you do it in under five minutes?

• Next time you go to a restaurant with your family, take your own water bottle with you! That way, if the waiter refills your water cup, you can take your water with you if you don't finish it at the table!

• There are hundreds of ways you can help save water—research some and encourage others to do the same!

Wildlife conservation is the practice of protecting wildlife and nature through science, action, and education. As the human population on earth grows, the wildlife population and their natural habitats decline. Wildlife is important in balancing the environment and the different processes in nature. Here are some ways you can help preserve wildlife:

• One of the best ways to get involved in wildlife conservation is to join a local organization—just like Joris! Try volunteering at a local animal shelter on weekends or see if there are larger organizations nearby you can join to help.

• Protect the small things. Try putting a spider outside instead of stomping on it inside. Just remember that everything—big or small—plays a role in nature, and it's important to protect it. Remind your friends to take care of nature too!

Environmental conservation is the practice of protecting the environment. The environment includes air, water, land, plants, and man-made things. Each part of our environment is important and plays a role in our lives, so it's important to protect it! Here are some ways you can help make the world a better place:

• Use less energy. Turn off the lights when you're not using them, don't sleep with the TV on, unplug things that aren't being used—these are all small things you can do to use less energy.

• Reduce, reuse, and recycle! You've heard this one before, but it really is the best way to help. Reduce your waste by being smart about what you throw away. Reuse things like plastic bags, and bring a reusable water bottle with you. Recycle anything that doesn't need to go into the trash bin.

Now that you've met some of the kids who are changing the world, what have you learned?

1. About how many people are homeless on a typical night in the United States?
a. 50,000   b. 1,000,000   c. more than 500,000

2. What did Natalie Hampton create?
a. "blessing bags"   b. a device called "Tethys"   c. an app called "Sit With Us"

3. Gitanjali Rao is from Flint, Michigan.
a. true   b. false

4. How old was Joris when he decided to help cheetahs?
a. six   b. two   c. five

5. About what percentage of water in the world is drinkable?
a. 98%   b. 1%   c. 5%

6. Wildlife conservation is the practice of protecting the wild nature inside you.
a. true   b. false

7. Which two amazing kids were honored with the Gloria Barron Prize for Young Heroes?
a. Joris and Jahkil   b. Joris and Natasha   c. Jahkil and Gitanjali

8. Who is the Greek goddess of fresh water?
a. Gitanjali   b. Tethys   c. Natalie

9. Which young inventor invented the folded paper bag?
a. Louis Braille   b. Margaret Knight   c. Joris Hutchison

10. Being kind is only helpful to others and not to yourself.
a. true   b. false